CELEBRATING THE FAMILY NAME OF LI

Celebrating the Family Name of Li

Walter the Educator

Silent King Books
a WhichHead Entertainment Imprint

Copyright © 2024 by Walter the Educator

All rights reserved. No part of this book may be reproduced in any manner whatsoever without written permission except in the case of brief quotations embodied in critical articles and reviews.

First Printing, 2024

Disclaimer

This book is a literary work; the story is not about specific persons, locations, situations, and/or circumstances unless mentioned in a historical context. Any resemblance to real persons, locations, situations, and/or circumstances is coincidental. This book is for entertainment and informational purposes only. The author and publisher offer this information without warranties expressed or implied. No matter the grounds, neither the author nor the publisher will be accountable for any losses, injuries, or other damages caused by the reader's use of this book. The use of this book acknowledges an understanding and acceptance of this disclaimer.

Celebrating the Family Name of Li is a memory book that belongs to the Celebrating Family Name Book Series by Walter the Educator. Collect them all and more books at WaltertheEducator.com

USE THE EXTRA SPACE TO DOCUMENT YOUR FAMILY MEMORIES THROUGHOUT THE YEARS

LI

Beneath the moon's eternal glow,

The name of Li begins to grow.

A melody sung by rivers wide,

A tale of strength and humble pride.

Rooted deep in ancient lore,

The name of Li forever soars.

A brushstroke bold, a symbol true,

A lineage vast as morning's dew.

In bamboo groves and mountain streams,

The Li name dances in poets' dreams.

Its syllables, a gentle breeze,

Whispering through the autumn trees.

From scholars' halls to warriors' might,

The Li name shines like stars at night.

Their wisdom guides, their honor stays,

A lantern bright through shadowed days.

The calligraphy of history's scroll,

Winds through the heart and fills the soul.

Each stroke of Li a story penned,

A legacy that will not end.

Farmers tilling fertile lands,

Crafting life with steady hands.

Merchants crossing ocean tides,

The Li name flows where hope abides.

A family vast, yet closely tied,

With roots that spread, yet unify.

Their laughter echoes, warm and free,

A bond unbroken, eternally.

Through storms they've weathered, calm they've stayed,

With courage fierce and kindness displayed.

In every heart, a flame burns bright,

Carried by those who bear Li's light.

Through art and song, through toil and grace,

The Li name finds its sacred place.

An endless thread in the world's great loom,

Weaving joy where flowers bloom.

So sing, oh world, of the name of Li,

A family bound by destiny.

Through time and space, they'll always be,

A shining emblem of unity.

ABOUT THE CREATOR

Walter the Educator is one of the pseudonyms for Walter Anderson. Formally educated in Chemistry, Business, and Education, he is an educator, an author, a diverse entrepreneur, and he is the son of a disabled war veteran. "Walter the Educator" shares his time between educating and creating. He holds interests and owns several creative projects that entertain, enlighten, enhance, and educate, hoping to inspire and motivate you. Follow, find new works, and stay up to date with Walter the Educator™

at WaltertheEducator.com

www.ingramcontent.com/pod-product-compliance
Lightning Source LLC
LaVergne TN
LVHW012051070526
838201LV00082B/3915